# LET'S GET
# FIZZICAL

 Penguin Random House

**Editor** Laura Bithell
**US Editor** Kayla Dugger
**Designer** Vanessa Hamilton
**Jacket Designer** Nicola Powling
**Managing Editor** Dawn Henderson
**Art Director** Maxine Pedliham
**Publishing Director** Mary-Clare Jerram
**Producer, Pre-production**
Heather Blagden
**Producer** Stephanie McConnell
**Photography** William Reavell
**Special Sales Creative**
**Project Manager** Alison Donovan

**Author** Pippa Guy

First American Edition, 2018
Published in the United States by
DK Publishing
1745 Broadway, 20th Floor,
New York, NY 10019

Copyright © 2018
Dorling Kindersley Limited
DK, a Division of Penguin
Random House LLC
22 11
015–311197–Nov/2018

A catalog record for this book is available
from the Library of Congress.
ISBN 978-1-4654-7388-2

Printed and bound in China

All images © Dorling Kindersley Limited

A WORLD OF IDEAS:
SEE ALL THERE IS TO KNOW

www.dk.com

# CONTENTS

# AUTHOR'S NOTE

**I FELL IN LOVE WITH** this industry because of my love of people and the social aspect that comes with a cocktail. A drink is so much more than a blend of ingredients; it's an experience of history, learning, creativity, and sociability.

As someone who's never had a detailed life plan, I tend to follow the ethos of do what makes you happy and you will end up in a job that makes you happy. I stumbled upon the wine and spirits industry as a student in Leeds trying to be more self-sufficient, and I haven't stopped working since. The industry is physically, mentally, and emotionally challenging, and it can be exhausting. But if you're up for the challenge, it can also be incredibly rewarding.

Approximately 3 years ago, I was offered an opportunity I couldn't resist. At the time, I was a working at legendary Leeds bar Oporto. I got talking to Declan McGurk, manager of the American Bar at The Savoy Hotel, and a few weeks later, he asked me to join his team. Since then, so many of my wildest dreams have come true. Under the patient teaching of head bartender Erik Lorincz, I now hold the position of senior bartender—the first female to take on such a role in a century. I have seen the bar itself grow, and I have witnessed and been a part of some of the most memorable achievements in its incredibly long history. In October 2017, it was crowned the "World's Best Bar."

A large part of that history comes from a man named Harry Craddock, head bartender of the American Bar in the 1920s and '30s. He created *The Savoy Cocktail Book*, probably the most important cocktail book of the 20th century and a text that has

guided bartenders globally for decades. It has been a huge pillar of my learning, and a great source of inspiration and wisdom when writing this book; you will see many references to it as you read through! From my own Pearfection spritz to the American Bar's Moonwalk, the following pages are a combination of three of my loves: cheesy puns, fizz, and cocktails …

**LET'S GET FIZZICAL!**

Where do the **bubbles** in sparkling wine come from? What's the difference between **brut** and **demi-sec?** Can you cheat with Cava instead of **Champagne?** Become a **fizz whiz** and get the lowdown on some of the **most popular** bubbly beverages—although there are **many more** sparkling wines from around the world to explore!

# A BEGINNER'S GUIDE TO BUBBLY

# HOW DO THEY **MAKE IT BUBBLY?**

**THE "SPARKLE" IN FIZZY WINES** is caused by carbon dioxide, a natural by-product of fermentation. Any fizz produced in winemaking is usually let loose to create still white or red wine, but some wines taste better with bubbles. To capture the sparkle, winemakers must stage an intervention, trapping and enhancing the bubbles in a tightly sealed bottle or tank.

## FERMENTATION

**AS THE SUGAR** is consumed by the yeast, alcohol is produced, along with carbon dioxide. The result is a dry (low-sugar) base wine.

aromas

$CO_2$

heat

alcohol

**Sugar**
This comes from the juice of the grapes. The grapes also contain acids and tannins (a bitter compound), which add to the flavor.

**Yeast**
Yeasts (microscopic organisms) occur naturally on grape skins, although they are often introduced artificially for better results.

**Alcohol**
The sugar is eaten by the yeast and converted into alcohol. Heat, aromas, and carbon dioxide are also produced.

# THE TRADITIONAL METHOD

**PIONEERED IN CHAMPAGNE,** this is the original way of making fizz and a marker of premium wine. It is a legal requirement that all Champagne is made via this method. It is a time-consuming, laborious, and expensive process, but it produces great results. Secondary fermentation occurs inside each individual bottle.

### 1. Base wine
A still base wine is made. This is fermented dry (with low sugar), often using underripe grapes.

### 2. Bottle and sweeten
With the addition of a little more sugar and yeast, the bottles of base wine are tightly sealed.

### 3. Secondary fermentation
This creates more carbon dioxide in the sealed bottle, carbonating the wine.

### 4. Autolysis (aging)
The lees (dead yeast particles) are left in the bottle for months or even years. Contact with the lees creates complexity.

### 5. Disgorging
After aging, the lees will have risen to the neck of the bottle. They are frozen so they can be easily removed as a block of ice.

### 6. Dosage
Before the wine is resealed, sugar (dosage) is added. The amount of sugar depends on the desired level of sweetness.

# THE TANK METHOD

**MANY FIZZY WINES** are now made via less time-consuming methods. In the "tank method," the aging stage is skipped because the wines are intended to be fresh and young. As the name suggests, the bubbles are created in a pressurized tank rather than in the bottle. The advantage of this method is that the wine can be produced in bulk. It is faster and more economical than the "traditional method."

# FIZZ KNOW-HOW

**TO MAKE** the best cocktails, you need to know exactly how to handle your fizz. Plus, having a few fun facts up your sleeve is a great way to amuse your guests while you make the drinks. It's time to brush up on your bubbly knowledge, become a fizz whiz, and put the pro in Prosecco.

## WHAT'S the best TEMPERATURE to STORE BUBBLY?

The general consensus is that most sparkling wines taste better when chilled, so your fridge should do the trick. Vintage Champagne is an exception—it is best stored in a cool room at 50–55°F (10–13°C).

## HOW do you OPEN BUBBLY SAFELY?

Be careful when opening fizz! Open the wire cage and, keeping your hand over the cork, twist the bottle to release. Don't twist the cork, and never open in the direction of another person or a breakable object!

## How MANY GRAPES GO INTO a BOTTLE of BUBBLY?

It takes approximately 600–800 grapes to make a single bottle of sparkling wine. When you think about the time and labor that goes into producing the fruit, it's no wonder a bottle of bubbly can get pricey!

## How MUCH PRESSURE does FIZZ CREATE?

The pressure in a bottle of Champagne is about two to three times the pressure in the tires of a car! This means fizz needs extra-thick bottles and corks to prevent it from exploding.

## WHICH FIZZ is WHICH?

**THE MOST** confusing fizz jargon is the terminology around the levels of sweetness. When Champagne was first made, it was sweetened with large amounts of sugar. Over time, a desire for dryer (less sweet) styles developed, and winemakers started adding less dosage (sugar). These wines were named "demi-sec" or "sec," meaning half-dry or dry. The demand for even drier wines increased, so they had to invent new terms that meant "drier than dry." This is how the word "brut" was born.

TO PUT IT SIMPLY, THE STYLES TRANSLATE AS BELOW:

- **BRUT NATURE:** Completely dry, with zero added sugar
- **EXTRA BRUT:** Extremely dry
- **BRUT:** Very dry; the most common style
- **EXTRA DRY:** Off-dry
- **SEC:** Slightly sweet
- **DEMI-SEC:** Sweet
- **DOUX:** The sweetest style of sparkling wine

### CAN I KEEP it FIZZY with a SPOON?

Sorry to burst your bubble, but this is an old wives' tale. Sticking a spoon in the top of your bottle of bubbly won't make it last any longer. Seal it with a Champagne stopper to retain the fizz.

### HOW LONG can I KEEP an OPEN BOTTLE?

Once opened, Prosecco and Cava should be consumed within 1–3 days. Champagne lasts a little longer—around 3–5 days. Your bottle of bubbly will be at its best on the day of opening.

### WHY do we SERVE FIZZ in CHAMPAGNE FLUTES?

Bubbly wines lose carbonation faster with a large surface area, so they are best served in tall, thin flutes. The long stem is designed to keep your hands off the main glass, so you don't warm up the drink with body heat.

# CHAMPAGNE

## FRANCE

METHOD: Traditional

**THE WORLD'S OLDEST** and most famous fizz is made exclusively in the Champagne region in France. To qualify for the Champagne label, the region, method, and grapes must all follow regulations. The exceptionally high demand for this sparkling wine gives it a slightly higher price tag. The driest (least sweet) of our fizz styles listed, nearly all Champagne is made in the "brut" style (meaning it has less than half a teaspoon of sugar per glass). With the smallest and most persistent bubbles, expect extra body and a buttery taste due to lees aging. Champagne also has naturally high and cleansing acidity.

## FLAVOR Profile

Fruit: 2/10

Acidity: 10/10

Alcohol: 5/10

Sweetness: 1/10

Atmosphere of pressure: ~100 PSI

*" A crisp yet complex fizz for those with more luxurious tastes "*

# THE LOWDOWN

## GRAPES

All Champagne is made with one or a combination of three permitted grapes: Chardonnay (white grape), Pinot Noir (red grape), and/or Pinot Meunier (red grape). This is a legal requirement of Champagne production.

## TASTE

Look out for flavors of brioche or toast, marzipan, nuts, citrus fruits, and stone fruits.

## STYLES

### NON-VINTAGE (NV)
House-style Champagne with no age statement. Made from a blend of fruit from different harvests to create consistency of style.

### BLANC DE BLANC
100% Chardonnay grapes.

### BLANC DE NOIRS
Only Pinot Noir and Pinot Meunier.

### ROSÉ
Pink in color (all grapes can be used).

### VINTAGE
Champagne with a specific age statement. Made using fruit from one specific year.

## BRANDS

- **Bollinger**
- **Dom Pérignon**
- **Moët & Chandon**
- **Pol Roger**
- **Ruinart**
- **Veuve Clicquot**

# PROSECCO

## ITALY

METHOD: Tank

**PROSECCO SALES HAVE** skyrocketed in recent years, largely thanks to the price tag. Classy but not as expensive as Champagne, it is seen by many as a great alternative fizz. So what's the difference? Prosecco is produced using the efficient and inexpensive tank method, rather than the traditional method. As a wine designed to be consumed young, the tank method allows Prosecco to showcase its clean and floral aromas. The name Prosecco comes from the small town in the north of Italy where it all began. The region was promoted to DOC (quality guarantee) and DOCG (highest quality guarantee) status in 2009.

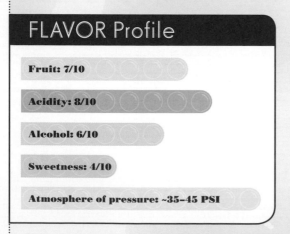

## FLAVOR Profile

Fruit: 7/10

Acidity: 8/10

Alcohol: 6/10

Sweetness: 4/10

Atmosphere of pressure: ~35–45 PSI

*" A light, easy-to-drink bubbly with subtle floral and pear notes "*

# THE LOWDOWN

 ## GRAPES

Prosecco is produced almost entirely from the white Glera grape variety (which used to be called Prosecco). Other grapes such as Perera, Bianchetta, and Verdiso can also be used, as well as some international varieties.

 ## TASTE

Look out for: apple, peach, and kiwi, with a creamy and uplifting floral finish.

 ## STYLES

### BRUT
This is the most common style.

### EXTRA DRY
Medium-dry or off-dry.

### DRY
Medium or medium-sweet.

### FRIZZANTE
If you see this label, it means the wine is semi-sparkling, rather than sparkling (spumante).

## BRANDS

- Zonin
- Terra Serena
- Mionetto
- Bisol
- Bottega

# CAVA

## SPAIN

METHOD: Traditional

CAVA IS THE MOST prolific sparkling wine produced in Spain. Cava must be produced in the traditional method, with a minimum of 9 months of aging on the lees to make the grade. It gets its name from the old caves used to store the bottles while they are aging. Unlike Champagne, the production of Cava is not limited to one geographical area. Around 90 percent of Cava comes from Penedès, Catalonia; however, Cava can also be produced in other parts of Spain, as long as it meets the regulations. Cava is not as expensive as Champagne, making it a more economical option for fizz lovers.

## FLAVOR Profile

Fruit: 6/10

Acidity: 8/10

Alcohol: 4/10

Sweetness: 3/10

Atmosphere of pressure: ~70–100 PSI

" A rich and appealingly affordable Spanish fizz "

# THE LOWDOWN

## GRAPES

Typical grapes used in the production of Cava are Macabeo (dominant), Parellada, and Xarel-Lo, although Chardonnay sometimes makes its way into the final blend.

## TASTE

Look out for greener flavors: celery, apple, grass, and lime, with a touch of brioche and almond.

## STYLES

### STANDARD
A minimum of 9 months of aging.

### RESERVA
A minimum of 15 months of aging.

### GRAN RESERVA
A minimum of 30 months of aging with an age statement.

### ROSADO
Pink in color.

**BRANDS**

- Anna de Codorníu
- Freixenet
- Agustí Torelló Mata
- Llopart
- Gramona

# ENGLISH SPARKLING

## UK, REGIONAL

**METHOD:** Traditional

**MAYBE NOT THE** first country that comes to mind when you're scanning stores for bubbly, but in recent years, the UK is really starting to live up to and even exceed other high-quality sparkling wines. With south coast soils found to have similar chalk levels to the Champagne region and Sussex boasting the most daylight hours in the UK, these ideal conditions are making high-quality English bubbly a real contender. As English sparkling wine production goes from strength to strength, we're starting to see more identity from the UK as they refine their style.

## GRAPES

The traditional Champagne grapes are used, as well as Seyval Blanc, Pinot Blanc, and Bacchus.

## TASTE

Expect aromatic and floral notes. Stone fruits, citrus, marzipan, and brioche from the lees aging via the traditional method.

## STYLES

English sparkling is made in the same styles as Champagne. These include Blanc de Blanc, Rosé, and Blanc de Noirs (*see p.13*).

**BRANDS**

- Bluebell
- Wiston
- Ridgeview
- Chapel Down
- Exton Park

# CALIFORNIA SPARKLING

## CALIFORNIA, SUBREGIONAL

**METHOD:** Traditional

**LIKE ENGLISH SPARKLING,** many California sparkling wines are essentially Champagne without the regional label. In fact, thanks to a law loophole, some California vineyards can even get away with using "champagne" to describe their wine, provided they list the place of origin, too. California has become the hub of US sparkling wine production, as the grapes are particularly suited to many of California's microclimates. The subtly different, riper flavor comes from the warmer, more fertile soils.

### GRAPES

The traditional Champagne grapes—Chardonnay, Pinot Noir, and Pinot Meunier—are most commonly used. Pinot blanc, Chenin blanc, and French Colombard can also be found in some California bubbly.

### TASTE

Crisp and dry with flavors of brioche, marzipan, nuts, citrus fruits, and orchard fruits. Small, light bubbles give a mousse finish. Slightly fruitier than Champagne.

### STYLES

California sparkling is made in the same styles as Champagne. These include Blanc de Blanc, Rosé, and Blanc de Noirs (see p.13).

**BRANDS**

- Domaine Chandon
- Mumm Napa
- Korbel
- Cook's
- André
- Schramsberg

# LAMBRUSCO

## ITALY

METHOD: Tank

**THIS IS RED FIZZ**. Largely underrated, Lambrusco is a fresh, light-bodied, red sparkling wine originating from northern Italy, just like Prosecco (except from a different region—namely Emilia-Romagna and Lombardy). Ranging from pale purple to deep red in color, this fruity and acidic fizz holds sweet berry flavors. Produced semi-sparkling, it is most often made dry or off-dry. In true Italian style, this wine benefits from being consumed alongside cheeses and cured meat!

## GRAPES

Predominantly Lambrusco Grasparossa, Lambrusco Maestri, Lambrusco Marani, Lambrusco Montericco, Lambrusco Salamino, and Lambrusco Sorbara.

## TASTE

Red and black cherry, blackberry, strawberry, boysenberry, mulberry, and rhubarb. Sharp acidity and a great food pairing.

## STYLES

- **LIGHTER:** A lighter style featuring Sorbara and Rosato grapes will appeal to a rosé drinker.
- **HEAVIER:** A heavier style featuring Grasparossa and Salamino grapes will appeal more to the red wine drinker.

**BRANDS**

- Villa Cialdini
- Marcello
- Civ & Civ
- Chiarli
- Paltrinieri

# MOSCATO D'ASTI

## ASTI, PIEDMONT, ITALY

**METHOD:** Tank

**MOSCATO D'ASTI** is a sweet, low alcohol sparkling wine made from the famous Moscato grape. Like all wines produced from this variety, they are typically fresh, extremely floral, and tropical in their flavor profile. Moscato wines rarely reach the heights of the fine wine sector, which makes them perfect for the sweet, lightly sparkling, inexpensive style produced in Piedmont, northwest Italy. "d'Asti" refers to the local township of Asti in the region; therefore, Moscato d'Asti directly translates to "Muscat from Asti."

### GRAPES
Moscato Bianco 100%.

### TASTE
Lightly effervescent with sweet peach, melon, apricot, and some pineapple flavors.

### STYLES
**N/A:** Moscato d'Asti is only produced in one sweet style.

**BRANDS**
- Govone
- Vietti
- Cascinetta
- Saracco
- Bartenura

# SWAP YOUR SPARKLE

SO YOU'VE GOT the lowdown on the different types of fizz, and you're now an expert on the key ingredient of your cocktails. But what if you can't get ahold of the right bottle of bubbly? Can you swap for Cava if your local supermarket is out of Prosecco? What do you do if your favorite recipe calls for Champagne, but you're planning a big party on a budget or you don't want to open that expensive vintage bottle? Luckily, there's usually room for a bit of fizz flexibility.

## COMPARISON CHART

|  | Champagne | Prosecco | Cava | English sparkling | California sparkling | Lambrusco | Moscato d'Asti |
|---|---|---|---|---|---|---|---|
| **WHERE'S IT FROM** | France | Italy | Spain | UK Regional | California | Italy | Italy |
| **FRUIT (/10)** | 2 | 7 | 6 | 2 | 3 | 8 | 9 |
| **ACIDITY (/10)** | 10 | 8 | 8 | 10 | 10 | 9 | 7 |
| **ALCOHOL (/10)** | 5 | 6 | 4 | 5 | 5 | 2 | 1 |
| **SWEETNESS (/10)** | 1 | 4 | 3 | 1 | 1 | 5 | 10 |
| **METHOD** | Traditional | Tank | Traditional | Traditional | Traditional | Tank | Tank |
| **PRESSURE (PSI)** | ~100 | ~35–45 | ~70–100 | ~70–90 | ~70–90 | ~30–60 | ~15 |

## I'M NOT on a CHAMPAGNE BUDGET

In a pinch, English sparkling, California sparkling, and Cava are all good Champagne swaps. They are made using the same method, and English sparkling and California sparkling even use the same grapes. The Cava grapes are slightly sweeter, but it is still a good swap. English sparkling comes from very similar soils to the Champagne region, so it would be the best choice of the three.

## The PROSECCO AISLE is EMPTY!

If you don't have a bottle of Prosecco on hand, Lambrusco makes a surprisingly good alternative. This fizz is growing in popularity every year, so you will likely see it more and more on the shelf. Like Prosecco, it has slightly larger, less refined bubbles than Champagne. It also shares similarities with Prosecco in terms of acidity and fruitiness.

## DOES it REALLY MATTER in a COCKTAIL?

This completely depends on the drink and your personal tastes. Most cocktails are traditionally made with a specific fizz, but that doesn't mean it will taste awful with something else. If you can't find a good swap listed here, why not experiment? A few exceptions, such as the Champagne Cocktail (pp.92–93), really should be served with their traditional bubbly.

**Master** the drink **mixing skills** to impress your guests and discover **professional** cocktail-making **tips and tricks**, from the essential lingo to the perfect glass shape. **Learn how** to pair **flavors**, how to get creative with ingredients, and how to present your **drinks with style**. Your **cocktail parties** will soon be unbeatable!

# GET THE PARTY STARTED

# COCKTAIL BASICS

OVER THE NEXT few pages, you'll delve into the details and learn everything you need to know to become a cocktail pro. If you're eager to dive straight into the recipes, why not consult this handy guide to get a handle on the basics first?

## How MANY DRINKS does each RECIPE MAKE?

Each recipe in this book makes one drink. This is traditional for cocktail recipes, as people tend to order different drinks, so bartenders are usually making one drink at a time. It also makes the math easy if you need to increase quantities.

## How FULL should my GLASS BE?

The general rule is to leave a two-finger gap for drinks served in a Champagne flute and a one-finger gap in other glasses. Avoid filling to the brim, as your drink will spill!

## DO I NEED a GARNISH?

Garnishes work best when they are relevant to the ingredients of the drink. However, you don't need to stick to the ones listed in the recipes—you can get as creative as you like or get rid of them altogether.

# LEARN the LINGO

## THE TECHNIQUES

Making a cocktail isn't as simple as just throwing all the ingredients together. Depending on the ingredients, there are a number of different preparation techniques:

- **BUILD** Each ingredient should be added directly to the serving glass.
- **SHAKE** Some or all of the ingredients are vigorously shaken in a cocktail shaker.
- **STIR** Some or all of the ingredients are stirred in a mixing glass with ice.
- **MUDDLE** Ingredient(s) should be mashed up into a pulp.
- **LIGHTLY MUDDLE** Ingredient(s) should be gently bruised to release flavors.
- **STRAIN** Stirred and shaken cocktails are always strained to ensure unwanted ice or ingredients don't go into the serving glass.
- **DOUBLE STRAIN** A fine strainer should be used with your normal strainer to catch any extra shards of ice or any tiny pieces of unwanted ingredients.

## THE INGREDIENTS

Aside from the bubbly, fruit juice, and spirits, there are a few more complex ingredients that may pop up in the recipes. These add flavor and help to balance the drink:

- **BITTERS** Intense and highly concentrated, bitters are alcoholic spirits with botanical flavorings. Used sparingly in cocktails to add complexity—a bit like salt and pepper in cooking!
- **SYRUP** A sweetening agent made from sugar, water, and often additional flavors, such as citrus.
- **PURÉE** A thick liquid made from blended fruit, often with added sugar.
- **INFUSION** A base liquid that has been rested with an ingredient to allow it to adopt the flavor.
- **LIQUEUR** A low-alcohol distilled spirit that has been infused with a flavor and sweetened.

## THE GARNISHES

A garnish shows off the flavor profile of a drink and adds a creative finish.

- **TWIST** A piece of citrus peel, lightly twisted to release oils and aromas. Make sure you remove the bitter pith. Placed decoratively on or in the drink.
- **SPRIG** A small top stem section of a herb with leaves or flowers. This part is the freshest and most aesthetically pleasing for garnishes.
- **ZEST** Grated peel from a citrus fruit. It adds flavor, as well as a burst of color.

- **RIM** Adding salt or sugar to the edge of the glass to add flavor and decoration. This also works well with edible glitter.
- **COIN** Essentially the same as a twist but smaller, circular, and subtler.
- **WEDGE** A slice of fruit. It adds flavor and bold color.
- **COCKTAIL STICK** A small, thin stick for skewering garnishes and displaying them in or across the glass.

# TOOLS AND EQUIPMENT

IF YOU WANT to throw a cocktail party or set up a home bar, you're going to need a good set of shiny tools. As well as producing delicious drinks, cocktail-making sets can be works of art. Buy a new matching set or keep an eye out in vintage and antique stores for the occasional gem. Some pieces of equipment are essential, while others will just make your life a little bit easier. The most important tools you need are a jigger, shaker, and bar spoon.

## 1. JIGGER

The most important piece of equipment, this fine measuring tool allows you to accurately measure even the smallest amounts. If you can find one with lined measurements on the inside, it's even more useful. Hold between your index and middle fingers and start by pouring very slowly until you get confident. This ensures that your measurements are accurate and your cocktails balanced.

## 2. SHAKER

You can either buy a three-piece shaker with a built-in strainer (as pictured) or a two-piece Boston shaker. The latter is made of two tins that slot together, and you'll need a separate strainer. For beginners, a three-piece is recommended, as they are a little easier to use.

## 3. BAR SPOON

This is used to stir your cocktails. The best bar spoons have a long, twisted handle, which allows you to stir between your middle and ring fingers with minimal movement.

## KEY

| | |
|---|---|
| **1** Jigger | **6** Muddler |
| **2** Shaker | **7** Hawthorne strainer |
| **3** Bar spoon | **8** Tongs |
| **4** Mixing glass or tin | **9** Juicer |
| **5** Fine strainer | **10** Peeler and zester |

**TOOLS AND EQUIPMENT CONTINUED ▶**

### 4. MIXING GLASS OR TIN

If necessary, this can be substituted with the bottom half of a shaker; however, a custom mixing glass with ease of stirring and a lip for pouring will make your experience a lot smoother. They are also incredibly elegant—a great mantelpiece decoration when not in use!

### 5. FINE STRAINER

Essentially, a very small sieve. We fine strain a cocktail with any little bits of fruit, seeds, leaves, or small shards of ice to prevent dilution. Use this alongside your Hawthorne strainer when the recipes call for "double straining."

### 6. MUDDLER

For mashing ingredients! Great to use with fresh fruit to extract juices or any herb to gently bruise to release flavor. Essentially the same as a pestle used in cooking.

### 7. HAWTHORNE STRAINER

When using a two-piece Boston shaker, this is your best friend for removing the liquid and leaving ice and unwanted ingredients in the tin. A spring coil will fit the top of nearly any shaker, holding back all the solid ingredients and only allowing the liquid through to your glass.

### 8. TONGS

For hygiene purposes. No matter how clean you think your hands are, please don't put them in your guest's drink. Use tongs. Work clean. Look elegant and professional.

## 9. JUICER

The explanation is in the name. Make sure to strain out any seeds and pulp where possible. Always juice fresh, either on the day if you're having a party or while making the drink.

## 10. PEELER AND ZESTER

A knife will do, but a peeler is a little simpler to use and cuts more rind with less pith—a lot harder to do with a knife alone. Peel and zest are components in many cocktails, so these tools will come in handy.

### the LAST STRAW

**ONCE GIVEN** away with almost every long cocktail, plastic straws seem set to become a thing of the past. If you prefer to drink with a straw, there are many alternative, environmentally friendly options out there. Colorful paper straws can double as a drink decoration, and bamboo straws make a good, sustainable choice. If you want something to last longer, many reusable straws are made from metal or flexible rubber and come complete with cleaning kits.

# SHAKEN, NOT STIRRED

**MANY COCKTAIL RECIPES** require the ingredients to be shaken in a cocktail shaker before serving. This technique doesn't just look impressive and give you a chance to use your new shiny cocktail mixing set; it helps blend the flavors and dilute and aerate (add air to) your drink. For a beginner, a three-piece shaker with a built-in strainer is a lot more user-friendly.

## TIP

**IF YOU** want to master a really great shake, practice with rice. Its weight helps improve your muscle memory, and the loud noise helps you create an even rhythm.

1. **ADD YOUR INGREDIENTS** to the shaker. If it's your first shaking attempt, start with the cheapest ingredient first. This is to avoid wasting expensive items if you make a mistake and have to start again.

2. **FILL YOUR SHAKER** halfway with ice, using tongs for hygiene purposes. Ice cubes are essential, as they cool and dilute the drink. They also make the distinctive loud rattling sound associated with cocktail shaking.

3. **HOLD THE SHAKER** in both hands and place your thumb over the top to ensure the top is tightly secured. Shake hard for the allocated time, usually 10–15 seconds, to thoroughly mix the flavors and to introduce air into the ingredients.

4. **STRAIN THE LIQUID** into a chilled glass. Some recipes may require you to "double strain" to ensure small pieces of ice and fruit are blocked from entering the glass. To do this, pour through a fine strainer, as well as the built-in strainer.

# STIR WITH STYLE

**SOME COCKTAIL RECIPES** require the ingredients to be stirred rather than shaken. This technique is gentler, introducing less water and air into the mixture and combining the ingredients in a less vigorous manner. It tends to be used for drinks with a light flavor and subtle ingredients—these won't benefit from extra dilution or air.

1. **FILL A CHILLED** mixing glass halfway with ice, using tongs for hygiene purposes.

2. **ADD YOUR INGREDIENTS** to the mixing glass. The order you choose to add these in won't affect the taste of the final drink, but you may want to start with the cheapest ingredients to avoid wasting expensive items if you make a mistake.

3. **USE A BAR SPOON** to stir the ingredients slowly for the allocated amount of time, usually 20-30 seconds, so that the drink is adequately mixed, chilled, and diluted. Keep the bar spoon touching the side of the glass as you stir.

4. **PLACE A STRAINER** on the top of your mixing glass and grip firmly in place. Pour the liquid from the mixing glass into your chilled glassware.

## TIP

**LIGHTLY HOLD** your bar spoon between your middle and ring fingers, with the others resting on the spoon for support. Use your ring finger to direct a clockwise motion.

# GLASS GALLERY

**CHOOSING GLASSWARE** is arguably one of the most exciting parts of making and creating a drink. Glasses come in all shapes, sizes, and designs, and they can really change the overall aesthetic of a cocktail. If you're looking for inspiration to expand your glassware collection, try browsing antique shops and secondhand stores. You may find some truly amazing and unique pieces.

## 1. CHAMPAGNE FLUTE

**THE CHAMPAGNE FLUTE** is used for bubbly cocktails that don't contain ice, such as Mimosas and Bellinis. Flutes come in a variety of styles, the glass on the left being the classic. The elegant, thin body is designed to prevent the bubbles from escaping.

## 2. MARTINI GLASS

**THIS GLASS, SOMETIMES** simply called a "cocktail glass," is also designed for mixed drinks that don't contain ice. It can hold more liquid than the flute, so it tends to be used for heavier cocktails with more ingredients. Handle carefully, as these glasses spill easily!

## 3. COUPE GLASS

**BEFORE THE FLUTE,** this was the traditional glass for drinking straight Champagne. It has now evolved into a classy glass for serving cocktails, the big surface area allowing the aromas to shine. It can be used interchangeably with the martini glass.

GLASS GALLERY CONTINUED  ▶

## 4. WINE GLASS

THIS GLASS IS THE BEST choice for any spritz-style drink that holds many components—for example, ice and larger volumes of liquid.

## 5. SMALL WINE OR SHERRY GLASS

HALFWAY BETWEEN a wine glass and a Champagne flute, these dainty glasses hold shorter, and often stronger, cocktails. They still have enough room for ice, if the recipe calls for it.

## 6. ROCKS GLASS

A SHORT, ROBUST glass with the ability to hold a relatively small volume of liquid, and therefore often used for strong cocktails. As the name suggests, you'd expect to find ice in a drink served in this glass.

## 7. HIGHBALL

A LONG GLASS with lots of room for ice and plenty of liquid. This style tends to be used to hold refreshing, light drinks that use a large amount of liquid mixer in proportion to the alcohol.

## 8. COCKTAIL MASON JAR

AN INCREASINGLY POPULAR style, you can now even find these with handles. If not, you can just reuse your old mason jars to liven up a summer get-together. This glass is suited to long drinks and is best used as an alternative to the highball glass.

## 9. COPPER MUG

MADE FAMOUS BY the Moscow Mule, the copper takes on and maintains the temperature of the ice, keeping your drink nice and cool.

# HOW TO MAKE SYRUPS AND PURÉES

**SYRUPS (SIMPLE OR FRUIT-FLAVORED)** and purées are used to sweeten, balance, and add flavor to drinks. If you're nifty in the kitchen and have a good palate for flavor pairing, you can get as creative as you'd like!

## PURÉE RECIPE

Purées not only add flavor and color, they also bring texture to a cocktail.

1. **WASH** and prepare the fresh fruit. Chop off any stalks and remove any pips or seeds.
2. **ADD** all ingredients to a blender and purée for 1 minute.
3. **STRAIN** through a fine sieve to catch any solids.
4. **BOTTLE** and store in the fridge for up to 5 days.

### BLUEBERRY PURÉE

This gives the Blueberry Bellini its striking color and delicious flavor *(pp.54-55)*.

**7 oz (200g) blueberries**
**7 fl oz (200ml) simple syrup**
**Juice of ¼ a lemon**

### STRAWBERRY PURÉE

This purée stars as a key ingredient in the Rossini *(pp.60-61)*.

**½ oz (15g) strawberries**
**3½ fl oz (100ml) simple syrup**
**Juice of ¼ a lemon**

### PEACH PURÉE

An essential component of the classic Bellini *(pp.52-53)*.

**1 white peach, peeled and pit removed**
**3½ fl oz (100ml) simple syrup**
**1 squeezed slice of lemon**

**CHEAT IT:** Blend canned peaches for a quick and easy alternative.

### PASSIONFRUIT PURÉE

This summery fruit adds an extra tropical hint to the Pornstar Martini *(pp.80-81)*.

**1 scooped passionfruit**
**1¾ fl oz (50ml) simple syrup**

Strain fruit before mixing with syrup.

### APPLE PURÉE

The fruity element in the Apple Bellini *(pp.54-55)*.

**1 apple, peeled and cored**
**3½ fl oz (100ml) simple syrup**

# SIMPLE SYRUP

Easy to make and found in many drinks, this simple syrup recipe is a cocktail-making staple.

1. **COMBINE** 3¹/₂ oz (100g) superfine sugar with 1²/₃ oz (50g) water over heat until dissolved.
2. **WAIT FOR** the mixture to cool, then transfer into a bottle and refrigerate.

# FLAVORED SYRUP RECIPE

You'll see sweet-flavored and fruity syrups pop up in several recipes. Why not experiment with your own flavors?

1. **WASH** and chop your fruit or other flavoring.
2. **ADD TO** a pan with the required amount of lemon juice, sugar, and water.
3. **BRING TO** a boil, then allow to simmer for 10 minutes or until the fruit has turned mushy.
4. **REMOVE FROM** the heat and allow to cool.
5. **STRAIN** the mixture through a fine sieve.
6. **BOTTLE** and refrigerate.
7. **USE WITHIN** a month.

**❝** *The majority of purées and syrups are now easy to buy premade; however, fresh always tastes better* **❞**

## WHITE PEPPER SYRUP

A syrup with a kick, used in the Strawberry Old Cuban *(pp.104–105)*.

**1 tsp white peppercorns**
**7 fl oz (200ml) simple syrup**

No need to heat this one! Simply combine and leave to infuse for 3 hours at room temperature, then strain.

## GINGER SYRUP (16 fl oz)

Combined with lemongrass paste, this gives the Lemongrass Mule its fiery kick *(pp.134–135)*.

**14 oz (400g) chopped and peeled ginger**
**9 oz (250g) sugar**
**16 fl oz (500ml) water**
**Juice of ½ a lemon**

CHEAT IT: Use premade ginger juice and mix with sugar over heat.

## RHUBARB SYRUP (16 fl oz)

Used for the Rhubarb Sgroppino *(pp.112–113)* and Midsummer Runner *(pp.132–133)*.

**14 oz (400g) chopped rhubarb**
**9 oz (250g) sugar**
**16 fl oz (500ml) water**
**Juice of ½ a lemon**

# HOW TO MAKE **INFUSIONS**

## WHY DO WE INFUSE SPIRITS?

Infusing alcohol adds an extra depth of flavor to really bring out the ingredients in a drink. It also allows us to subtly add ingredients that would be very difficult to mix with. Infusing at home is easy and can be a great way to impress guests at your next cocktail party.

### YOU WILL NEED

1 sealable jar
1 liquid measuring cup
1 strainer
1 labeled bottle to store your infusion
Base spirit
Flavoring of choice

**1. Measure out your** base spirit, then measure out your ingredients and add to the jar. For 16 fl oz (500ml) rosemary gin, use 4–5 fresh rosemary sprigs.

**2. Fill the jar** with your base spirit and seal tightly. Leave the mixture to infuse at room temperature for the correct amount of time. Rosemary gin needs 3 hours to infuse.

## OTHER INFUSIONS

| Spirit | Infusion | Quantities | Infusion time |
|---|---|---|---|
| **GIN**<br>This spirit works especially well with herbal and floral infusions. | Lavender Gin (see Lavender 75, pp.78-79) | 7 fl oz (200ml) gin<br>2 sprigs dried lavender | 3 hours |
| | Rose Petal Gin (see Rose 75, pp.78-79) | 7 fl oz (200ml) gin<br>$1/8$ oz (5g) dried rose petals | 3 hours |
| **VODKA**<br>A great choice for infusions, as the base spirit is relatively flavorless. | Citrus and Rose Vodka (see English Summer Rose, pp.136-137) | 16 fl oz (500ml) vodka<br>$2/5$ oz (12.5g) dried rose petals<br>Peels of 1 orange, 1 lemon, 1 lime, and 1 grapefruit | Citrus peels for 1.5 hours, then remove; dried roses for the full 3 hours |

**3. When finished** infusing, strain the liquid into a bottle. Use a cup with a lip to ensure accuracy—your liquid measuring cup from earlier will work well.

**4. Label the bottle** and seal your infusion tightly if you're not using it right away. To maximize shelf life, store your infusion in the fridge. It's best to use it within a month.

# FIZZ FLAVOR CHART

**IF YOU'RE LOOKING FOR** food flavors to complement your drink, or if you want to go one step further and come up with creative ideas for your own cocktails, this flavor chart is a great starting point. Try something from the list, or use the chart as inspiration to come up with your own combinations. There are many other flavors to experiment with!

## THE BEST FOR THE REST

- **ENGLISH SPARKLING WINE:** Take a look at the Champagne section of the chart for the best flavor combinations.

- **CALIFORNIA SPARKLING WINE:** Look to the Champagne section of the chart for flavors that may work well with this wine.

- **LAMBRUSCO:** Try sweet and fruity flavors, such as cherries or cream. Many Prosecco flavors will also work well with this red sparkling wine.

- **MOSCATO D'ASTI:** Nutty flavors, such as pistachio and coconut, work well. As with most bubblies, you can't go wrong combining with mint, peach, and orange.

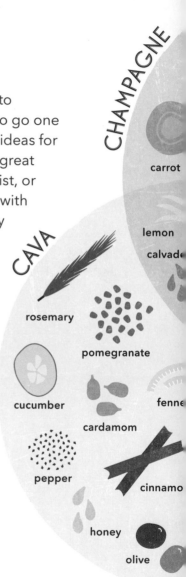

CHAMPAGNE

CAVA

carrot

lemon

calvad

rosemary

pomegranate

cucumber

fenne

cardamom

pepper

cinnamo

honey

olive

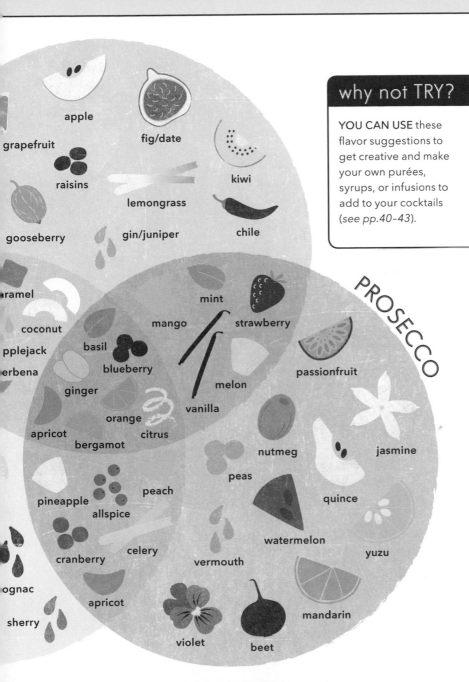

apple

fig/date

grapefruit

raisins

kiwi

lemongrass

gooseberry

gin/juniper

chile

## why not TRY?

**YOU CAN USE** these flavor suggestions to get creative and make your own purées, syrups, or infusions to add to your cocktails (*see pp.40–43*).

ramel

mint

coconut

mango

strawberry

pplejack

basil

erbena

blueberry

passionfruit

ginger

melon

vanilla

apricot

orange

citrus

bergamot

nutmeg

jasmine

peas

pineapple

peach

quince

allspice

celery

watermelon

yuzu

cranberry

vermouth

ognac

apricot

mandarin

sherry

violet

beet

PROSECCO

# SUMMER SPARKLE

Ah, summer—long days full of sunshine and the most enjoyable season for drinking cocktails outdoors with friends or hosting boozy barbecues. Light and refreshing, here are the top 5 picks for fizz cocktails to enjoy in the glorious warm weather.

**1** APEROL SPRITZ (*pp.56–57*) Spritzes are designed for summer sipping—the Aperol Spritz is the ultimate refresher.

**2** SPARKLING FRENCH MARTINI (*pp.120–121*) Full of fruity flavors, you'll feel like you've been transported to a tropical beach.

**3** PROSECCO MOJITO (*pp.88–89*) This long, minty

drink will keep you cool on a hot summer's day.

**4** SOUTHSIDE ROYALE (*pp.126–127*) The mint combined with the tart lemon makes for a refreshing drink.

**5** SGROPPINO (*pp.110–111*) Nothing says summer like fresh lemons and ice-cold sorbet.

# MAKING A SUMMER PUNCH

**A METHOD OF** mixing drinks that predates the cocktail, you can make almost any cocktail into a punch by increasing the volume. Try this recipe for the English Summer Rose (*pp.136–137*).

## TO SERVE 15:

15 FL OZ (450ml) vodka infused with citrus and rose
15 FL OZ (450ml) lemon juice
7½ FL OZ (225ml) simple syrup
4 TBSP (45 drops) blossom bitters
14 FL OZ (400ml) rosé Champagne

**FILL YOUR PUNCH BOWL** with ice, pour all ingredients over the top, then stir. You can then have fun decorating your party showpiece with edible flowers, citrus peels, or rose petals.

# FESTIVE FIZZ

Winter, the season of sparkle and making merry—naturally, a perfect occasion for drinking. But what makes a good festive cocktail? Whether it's full of warming flavors or an elegant celebration tipple, here are the top 5 winter fizz cocktail picks.

**1** MIMOSA (*pp.62–63*)
A light option to start off a long day of festive celebrations.

**2** DEATH IN THE AFTERNOON (*pp.122–123*) A touch of absinthe will keep you warm in the winter months.

**3** CYNAR FIZZ (*pp.140–141*)
A heavier drink is a welcome distraction from cold weather.

**4** KIR ROYALE (*pp.98–99*)
With rich, warm colors and an equally rich flavor, this drink makes a classy choice for your winter cocktail party.

**5** TWINKLE (*pp.84–85*)
A modern classic. This elegant cocktail is a huge crowd pleaser and the ultimate celebration drink.

# SUGAR AND SPARKLE

**WHY NOT JAZZ UP** your drink with a sweet, frosty decoration? This trick also works for an edible glitter or salt rim.

## SUGARING THE RIM OF A GLASS

1. Make sure your chosen glass is clean and dry.
2. Pour sugar into a small bowl or plate so that it is easily accessible.
3. Cut a slice of lemon or lime.
4. With the glass upside down, gently rub the citrus slice around the rim of the glass so that it is left slightly damp.
5. Roll the glass gently in the sugar.
6. Use a napkin over your finger to gently tidy the edges, ensuring there is no sugar left on the inside of the glass.

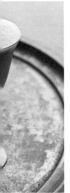

**Always popular** for boozy brunches, classy holiday **celebrations**, and long summer afternoons, these are light, **refreshing** drinks that go down far too easily. From the sophisticated peach **Bellini** to delicious **new inventions**, you definitely won't be short on exciting **cocktail ideas** for your next event.

# BELLINIS, MIMOSAS, & SPRITZES

# BELLINI

It may seem like the latest brunch trend, but sophisticated aristocrats were sipping Bellinis as early as the 1940s. This fruity drink was invented by Giuseppe Cipriani, founder of Harry's Bar in Venice, and was inspired by the work of 15th-century Venetian artist Giovanni Bellini. The Bellini rivals the Aperol Spritz as the quintessential summer drink.

## the CLASSIC RECIPE

Make your purée just before serving or on the same day for freshness.

1. Put ice into a mixing glass.
2. Add ⅘ fl oz (25ml) peach purée and top with 3½ fl oz (100ml) Prosecco.
3. Stir slowly for 15 seconds.
4. Strain into a Champagne flute.
5. Top with extra Prosecco, if necessary.

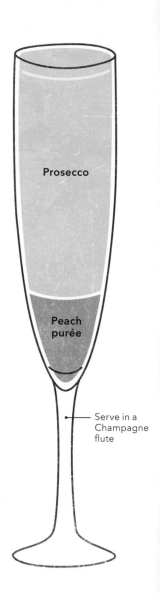

Prosecco

Peach purée

Serve in a Champagne flute

TURN THE PAGE FOR REINVENTIONS ▶

## LOSE the BOOZE

**Swap the Prosecco** for sparkling grape juice for a refreshing, nonalcoholic drink. Try this with the classic or either variation.

# **BELLINI** REINVENTED

## **BLUEBERRY BELLINI**

The delicious blueberry purée gives this variation a pop of color.

1. Put ice into a mixing glass.

2. Add the blueberry purée, then pour Prosecco over the top.

3. Stir slowly for 15 seconds.

4. Strain into a Champagne flute. Top with extra Prosecco, if necessary.

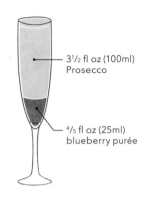

3¹/₂ fl oz (100ml) Prosecco

⁴/₅ fl oz (25ml) blueberry purée

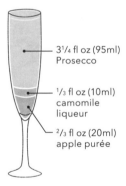

3¹/₄ fl oz (95ml) Prosecco

¹/₃ fl oz (10ml) camomile liqueur

²/₃ fl oz (20ml) apple purée

## **APPLE BELLINI**

A softer-tasting twist on the classic Bellini, perfect for lazy summer days.

1. Put ice into a mixing glass.

2. Add the apple purée and camomile liqueur.

3. Pour Prosecco over the top and stir slowly for 15 seconds.

4. Strain into a Champagne flute. Top with extra Prosecco, if necessary.

# APEROL SPRITZ

This cocktail is the quintessential Italian aperitif. Aperol, a bitter, citrus-flavored liqueur, was invented by the Barbieri brothers in Padua in 1919 and first combined with soda water and dry Prosecco to make this famous spritz in the 1950s. It is the perfect light, refreshing drink for a summer's day.

Soda water (optional)

Prosecco

Ice

Aperol

Serve in a wine glass

## the CLASSIC RECIPE

With or without soda water? Both versions taste great, so it's up to you.

1. Fill a red wine glass with ice cubes.
2. Add 2 fl oz (60ml) Aperol.
3. Top with Prosecco.
4. Add soda water for a lighter drink.

## LOSE the
# BOOZE

**Replace the Aperol** with rhubarb syrup, then top up your drink with equal parts soda water and lemonade.

### EXTRAS

**Garnish:** This drink wouldn't be complete without a fresh orange wedge.

# ITALICUS SPRITZ

An Italian liqueur that lends itself perfectly to a spritz, Italicus is classified as a Rosolio, a traditional Italian drink made with rose petals. Launched in 2016 and invented by Giuseppe Gallo, the zingy liqueur was inspired by a 19th-century family recipe and is becoming increasingly popular worldwide. Light, citrusy, and refreshing, this new bergamot gem will brighten any afternoon drinks.

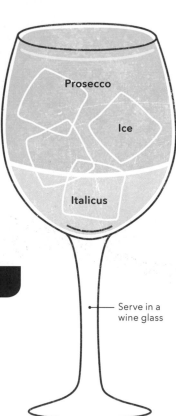

Prosecco

Ice

Italicus

Serve in a wine glass

## the CLASSIC RECIPE

The bubbly of choice, Prosecco, makes for a truly Italian experience.

1. Fill a red wine glass with ice cubes.
2. Add 2 fl oz (60ml) Italicus.
3. Top with Prosecco.

## EXTRAS

**Garnish:** A cocktail pick with a few olives makes an elegant garnish for this drink.

# ROSSINI

Named after the 19th-century Italian composer Gioachino Rossini, this strawberry alternative to the peach Bellini is so popular, it has become a classic in its own right. It makes a great celebration drink for the holiday season or New Year's Eve.

## the CLASSIC RECIPE

The strawberry purée gives this cocktail a striking red color.

1. Put ice into a mixing glass.
2. Add ⁴/₅ fl oz (25ml) strawberry purée and top with 3¹/₂ fl oz (100ml) Prosecco.
3. Stir slowly for 15 seconds.
4. Strain into a Champagne flute.
5. Top with extra Prosecco, if necessary.

Prosecco

Strawberry purée

Serve in a Champagne flute

## EXTRAS

**Garnish:** For a bit of festive flair, rim the glass with sugar and edible glitter.

SEE PP.48-49

# MIMOSA

A classic brunch favorite, this drink is delightfully simple. The Mimosa is comprised of equal parts Champagne and orange juice. It is slightly softer on the alcohol than its relative the Buck's Fizz, making it perfect for long summer days. It is said to have been invented by Frank Meier in 1925 at the Hôtel Ritz Paris.

## the CLASSIC RECIPE

Champagne is the traditional fizz, but other sparkling wines will also work well.

1. Make sure both ingredients are chilled.
2. Fill a Champagne flute halfway with Champagne.
3. Fill the second half of the glass with orange juice, leaving a two-finger-width gap at the top.

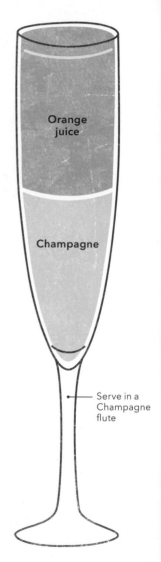

Orange juice

Champagne

Serve in a Champagne flute

## EXTRAS

**Garnish:** Add an elegant flourish with an orange twist garnish.

TURN THE PAGE FOR REINVENTIONS ▶

LOSE the
BOOZE

**Swap the Champagne** for lemonade or ginger ale. Try this with the classic recipe or any of the variations.

# MIMOSA REINVENTED

### POINSETTIA

A colorful twist with a sharper taste.

1. Make sure both ingredients are chilled.
2. Fill a Champagne flute halfway with Champagne.
3. Fill the second half with cranberry juice.

Half a glass cranberry juice

Half a glass Champagne

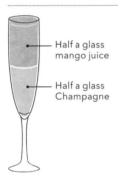

Half a glass mango juice

Half a glass Champagne

### MANGO MIMOSA

A tropical reinvention of the classic recipe.

1. Make sure both ingredients are chilled.
2. Fill a Champagne flute halfway with Champagne.
3. Fill the second half with mango juice.

### CARROT MIMOSA

An earthy, more experimental alternative.

1. Make sure both ingredients are chilled.
2. Fill a Champagne flute halfway with Champagne.
3. Fill the second half with carrot juice.

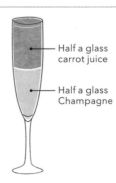

Half a glass carrot juice

Half a glass Champagne

# MEDITERRANEAN
## SPRITZ

This drink is a Spanish afternoon in a glass—deliciously citrusy, nutty, and fragrant. The gin is infused with rosemary for a hint of herbal flavor. This cocktail works particularly well with Gin Mare, a gin that also takes its inspiration from the sunny Mediterranean.

Cava

Ice

Orgeat

Lemon juice

Rosemary-infused gin

Serve in a wine glass

## the AUTHOR'S RECIPE

You'll need a few hours of preparation to infuse the gin; see pp.42-43.

1. Pour 1 fl oz (30ml) rosemary-infused gin, 1 fl oz (30ml) lemon juice, and 1/2 fl oz (15ml) orgeat into a shaker.
2. Add ice and shake thoroughly for 15 seconds.
3. Strain into a wine glass filled with ice.
4. Top with Cava.

## EXTRAS

**Garnish:** Decorate
this drink with a
lemon wedge and
a rosemary sprig.

# CAMPARI SPRITZ

This bright red spritz is a refreshing summer classic and a feast for the eyes. A bitterer alternative to the Aperol Spritz, the Campari Spritz will channel your inner Italian with a touch more dryness and a slightly higher alcohol content. It pairs delightfully with light, salty predinner appetizers such as pretzels and olives.

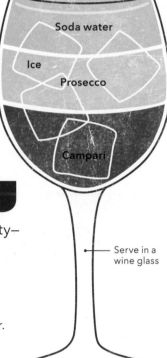

Soda water

Ice

Prosecco

Campari

Serve in a wine glass

## the CLASSIC RECIPE

This cocktail's beauty is in its simplicity—it makes a great, easy party drink.

1. Fill a wine glass with ice cubes.
2. Add 2 fl oz (60ml) Campari.
3. Top with half Prosecco and half soda water.

## EXTRAS

**Garnish:** An orange wedge or fresh raspberries make a great decoration.

# BLUSH SPRITZ

A sparkling interpretation of the classic Garibaldi, the key to this drink is the freshness of the juice. Buy freshly squeezed orange juice rather than concentrate, or even juice fresh oranges at home if you're feeling adventurous. If you're after a seriously frothy texture, blend the orange juice and Campari before adding the Prosecco.

## the AUTHOR'S RECIPE

Ensure all ingredients are chilled before you begin.

1. Pour 1²/₃ fl oz (50ml) Campari and 3¹/₂ fl oz (100ml) fresh orange juice into a shaker.
2. Fill with ice and shake for 10 seconds, then strain into a highball glass.
3. Top with chilled Prosecco and stir.

Serve in a highball glass

Prosecco

Fresh orange juice

Campari

## EXTRAS

**Garnish:** An orange wedge complements the citrus flavor of this drink.

# PEARFECTION

A boozy French-inspired spritz alternative, the star ingredient of this cocktail is a colorless French brandy, eau de vie, which literally translates as "water of life." To add an extra kick at the bottom of the glass, infuse the grapes in pear eau de vie for a day before adding them to your drink.

## the AUTHOR'S RECIPE

This light drink is full of fruity flavor and aroma.

1. Gently place two infused grapes at the bottom of a Champagne flute.
2. Pour 1/3 fl oz (10ml) pear eau de vie into the flute.
3. Top with Champagne.

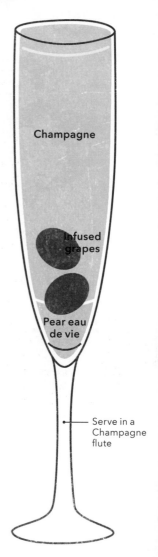

Champagne

Infused grapes

Pear eau de vie

Serve in a Champagne flute

## LOSE the
# BOOZE

**Replace the alcohol** with a combination of white grape juice and ginger ale. Use fresh, uninfused grapes.

**Classic cocktails** such as the **French 75** never seem to go out of fashion, while some newer **fizz** drinks are so popular, they are quickly becoming **modern classics**. Learn how to perfect these bubbly cocktails and discover **the story** behind them. With creative reinventions of many recipes, add an interesting **twist** to your **next party**!

# CLASSIC COCKTAILS & TWISTS

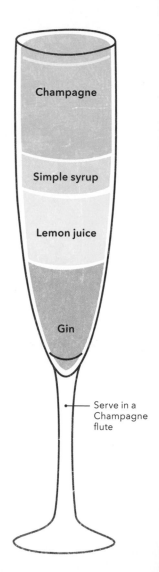

# FRENCH 75

The French 75 is one of the most popular celebration cocktails for weddings, birthdays, New Year's Eve, or just because it's Friday. It can be traced back to the Parisian New York Bar in 1915, the name inspired by the comparable kick of the French 75mm howitzer gun. This drink made its first published appearance in *The Savoy Cocktail Book* in 1930.

## the CLASSIC RECIPE

This cocktail brings out the best flavors of its simple ingredients.

1. Add 1 fl oz (30ml) gin, 1 fl oz (30ml) lemon juice, and ½ fl oz (15ml) simple syrup to a shaker.
2. Fill with ice and shake vigorously for 15 seconds.
3. Strain into a Champagne flute.
4. Top slowly with Champagne.

Champagne

Simple syrup

Lemon juice

Gin

Serve in a Champagne flute

## EXTRAS

**Garnish:** Jazz up your drink with a candied cherry or a lemon twist.

TURN THE PAGE FOR REINVENTIONS ▶

LOSE the
BOOZE

**Replace the gin** with
Seedlip nonalcoholic
distilled spirit and top
with soda water rather
than Champagne.

# FRENCH 75 REINVENTED

## ROSE 75

An elegant, floral variation on the classic.

1. Combine all ingredients except the Champagne in a shaker.

2. Fill the shaker with ice and shake vigorously for 15 seconds.

3. Strain into a Champagne flute, top with rosé Champagne, and garnish with rose petals.

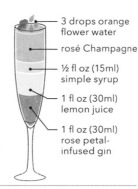

- 3 drops orange flower water
- rosé Champagne
- ½ fl oz (15ml) simple syrup
- 1 fl oz (30ml) lemon juice
- 1 fl oz (30ml) rose petal-infused gin

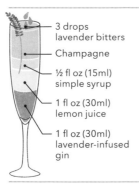

- 3 drops lavender bitters
- Champagne
- ½ fl oz (15ml) simple syrup
- 1 fl oz (30ml) lemon juice
- 1 fl oz (30ml) lavender-infused gin

## LAVENDER 75

The French 75 with an aromatic twist.

1. Combine all ingredients except the Champagne in a shaker.

2. Fill the shaker with ice and shake vigorously for 15 seconds.

3. Strain into a flute, top with Champagne, and garnish with a lavender sprig.

## GINGER 75

A twist for those who like a bolder flavor.

1. Combine all ingredients except the Champagne in a shaker.

2. Fill the shaker with ice and shake vigorously for 15 seconds.

3. Strain into a flute, top with Champagne, and garnish with a slice of fresh ginger.

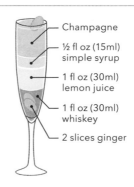

- Champagne
- ½ fl oz (15ml) simple syrup
- 1 fl oz (30ml) lemon juice
- 1 fl oz (30ml) whiskey
- 2 slices ginger

# PORNSTAR MARTINI

The pinnacle of modern classics, the Pornstar Martini was created as recently as 2002 by Douglas Ankrah at The Townhouse in Knightsbridge, London. Fabulously fruity and fun, this drink has become one of the most globally renowned fizz cocktails. Now you can enjoy this happy hour favorite at home.

Prosecco
Passionfruit purée
Pineapple juice
Simple syrup
Lemon juice
Vanilla vodka

Serve in a martini glass

## the CLASSIC RECIPE

The Prosecco can be served in a separate shot glass to sip on the side.

1. Pour 1⅓ fl oz (40ml) vanilla vodka, 1 fl oz (30ml) lemon juice, ½ fl oz (15ml) simple syrup, ⅔ fl oz (20ml) pineapple juice, and ½ fl oz (15ml) passionfruit purée into a shaker.

2. Fill with ice, shake for 10 seconds, and strain into a large martini glass.

3. Top with Prosecco, or serve Prosecco as a shot on the side.

## EXTRAS

**Garnish:** This drink wouldn't be complete without its signature half passionfruit garnish.

TURN THE PAGE FOR REINVENTIONS ▶

# **PORNSTAR** MARTINI
## REINVENTED

### **WATERMELON PORNSTAR**

Slightly less intense than the classic, this drink makes a great summer punch.

1. Combine all ingredients except the Prosecco and garnish in a shaker.

2. Fill with ice and shake for 10 seconds.

3. Strain into a martini glass and top with Prosecco. Garnish with a watermelon wedge.

Prosecco

¹/₂ fl oz (15ml) Chambord

²/₃ fl oz (20ml) watermelon juice

¹/₂ fl oz (15ml) simple syrup

1 fl oz (30ml) lemon juice

1¹/₃ fl oz (40ml) vanilla vodka

Prosecco

¹/₂ fl oz (15ml) passionfruit purée

²/₃ fl oz (20ml) pineapple juice

¹/₂ fl oz (15ml) simple syrup

1 fl oz (30ml) lemon juice

1¹/₃ fl oz (40ml) peated whisky

### **PEATSTAR MARTINI**

A simple yet brave variation on the original. Not for those with a subtle palate, it comes with a hint of smoke.

1. Combine all ingredients except Prosecco and garnish in a shaker.

2. Fill with ice and shake for 10 seconds.

3. Strain into a martini glass and top with Prosecco. Garnish with a half passionfruit.

# TWINKLE

The ultimate celebration cocktail, the Twinkle was created in 2002 by Tony Conigliaro. It may be a relatively recent invention, but this outrageously delicious drink seems set to stand the test of time. Floral, bubbly, and often served with a delicate lemon garnish or glittery finish, the Twinkle is the perfect way to welcome in the New Year.

## the CLASSIC RECIPE

Watch out—this drink is deceptively heavy on the booze!

1. Add ⁴/₅ fl oz (25ml) vodka and ½ fl oz (15ml) elderflower liqueur to a shaker.
2. Fill the shaker with ice and shake for 10 seconds.
3. Strain into a Champagne flute.
4. Top slowly with Champagne.

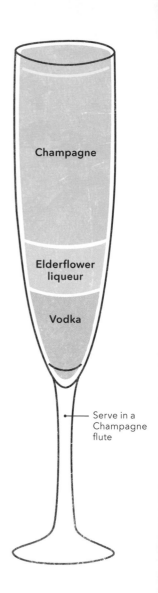

Champagne

Elderflower liqueur

Vodka

Serve in a Champagne flute

## LOSE the BOOZE

**Elderflower syrup** topped with sparkling apple juice turns this boozy drink into a fruity mocktail.

### EXTRAS

**Garnish:** Sprinkle edible glitter into the glass to really make your drink sparkle.

# NEGRONI SBAGLIATO

A Negroni is a classic gin cocktail, and "sbagliato" is the Italian word for mistake. The story goes that this drink was born when bartender Mirko Stocchetti accidentally poured Prosecco instead of gin into his Negroni. The popularity of this bubbly blunder will forever signify that sometimes you really do learn from your mistakes.

## the CLASSIC RECIPE

The sweet vermouth in this drink offsets the bitterness of the Campari.

1. Pour 1 fl oz (30ml) each of Campari and sweet vermouth into an ice-filled mixing glass.

2. Stir for 10 seconds.

3. Strain into a rocks glass filled with ice.

4. Top with Prosecco and stir again. Do this slowly to ensure the Prosecco stays bubbly.

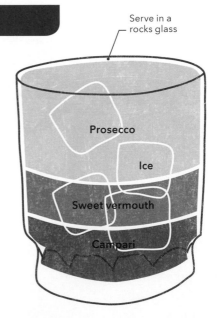

Serve in a rocks glass

Prosecco

Ice

Sweet vermouth

Campari

## EXTRAS

**Garnish:**
Freshen up this
drink with an
orange twist.

# PROSECCO MOJITO

The classic mojito is a drink so old, its history is a blur. It can be traced back to a 16th-century Cuban recipe for an "El Draque" named after the famous sea captain, Sir Francis Drake. This version with Prosecco appeals to lovers of a fresh, long fizz drink. The cool mint makes for easy summer sipping.

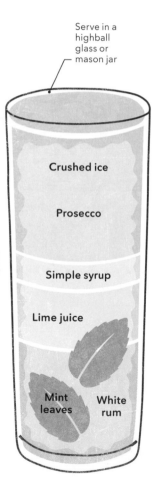

Serve in a highball glass or mason jar

Crushed ice

Prosecco

Simple syrup

Lime juice

Mint leaves

White rum

## the CLASSIC RECIPE

Present your drink in a tall, clear glass to really show off the ingredients.

1. Combine 2 fl oz (60ml) white rum, 6 mint leaves, 1 fl oz (30ml) lime juice, and ½ fl oz (15ml) simple syrup in a highball glass or mason jar.
2. Muddle with one scoop of crushed ice.
3. Add another scoop of crushed ice.
4. Top with Prosecco.

## LOSE the
# BOOZE

**For a nonalcoholic** option, replace the rum with apple juice and top up your drink with ginger ale.

## EXTRAS

**Garnish:** Boost the aroma of your cocktail with a decorative mint sprig.

**TURN THE PAGE FOR REINVENTIONS ▶**

# PROSECCO MOJITO
## REINVENTED

### SPARKLING PASSIONFRUIT MOJITO

The passionfruit adds some extra zing.

1. Muddle the mint, rum, lime juice, simple syrup, and passionfruit in a highball glass.

2. Top with Prosecco, then add crushed ice.

3. Garnish with a half passionfruit or mint.

Crushed ice
Prosecco
scooped ½ passionfruit
½ fl oz (15ml) simple syrup
1 fl oz (30ml) lime juice
2 fl oz (60ml) rum
6 mint leaves

Prosecco
Crushed ice
½ fl oz (15ml) simple syrup
1 fl oz (30ml) lemon juice
3 raspberries
2 fl oz (60ml) vanilla vodka
6 mint leaves

### SPARKLING RASPBERRY MOJITO

Best with fresh raspberries in late summer.

1. Muddle the mint, vanilla vodka, raspberries, lemon juice, and simple syrup in a highball glass.

2. Top with Prosecco, then add crushed ice.

3. Garnish with raspberries or mint.

### SPARKLING THYME MOJITO

A twist with herbal, subtle flavors.

1. Lightly muddle the thyme, vanilla vodka, lime juice, simple syrup, and peach purée in a highball glass.

2. Top with Prosecco, then add crushed ice.

3. Garnish with a sprig of thyme.

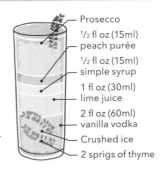

Prosecco
½ fl oz (15ml) peach purée
½ fl oz (15ml) simple syrup
1 fl oz (30ml) lime juice
2 fl oz (60ml) vanilla vodka
Crushed ice
2 sprigs of thyme

# CHAMPAGNE COCKTAIL

This is not just a Champagne cocktail—this is *the* Champagne cocktail. The recipe can be traced back to 1862, making it one of the true pioneers in mixing cocktails with Champagne and the inspiration for many other fizz drinks. Biscuit and cereal notes of Champagne are integral to the flavor—Prosecco simply won't do!

Serve in a coupe glass

Champagne

Sugar cube

Brandy

Angostura bitters

## the CLASSIC RECIPE

Slightly sweet yet very bold, this drink makes a great winter warmer.

1. Place the sugar cube in the center of the glass.
2. Cover with 5 drops Angostura bitters.
3. Add 4/5 fl oz (25ml) brandy.
4. Top with Champagne.

## EXTRAS

**Garnish:** Jazz up your drink with a floating "coin" of orange peel.

TURN THE PAGE FOR REINVENTIONS ▶

# CHAMPAGNE COCKTAIL
## REINVENTED

### MOONWALK

Created for the *Apollo 11* astronauts by Joe Gilmore of the Savoy Hotel's American Bar.

1. Stir bitters, flower water, and Grand Marnier in an ice-filled mixing glass for 20 seconds.

2. Strain into a Champagne flute with a sugar cube at the bottom.

3. Top with Champagne and garnish with an orange twist.

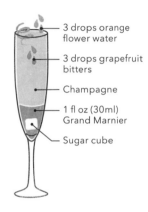

3 drops orange flower water

3 drops grapefruit bitters

Champagne

1 fl oz (30ml) Grand Marnier

Sugar cube

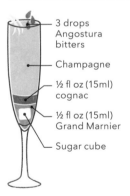

3 drops Angostura bitters

Champagne

½ fl oz (15ml) cognac

½ fl oz (15ml) Grand Marnier

Sugar cube

### PRINCE OF WALES

An interesting middle ground between the Moonwalk and classic Champagne Cocktail.

1. Stir bitters, cognac, and Grand Marnier in an ice-filled mixing glass for 20 seconds.

2. Strain into a Champagne flute with a sugar cube at the bottom.

3. Top with Champagne and garnish with a sprinkling of lemon zest.

# VALENCIA COCKTAIL NO.2

Aromatic and zesty, this classic drink from *The Savoy Cocktail Book* is a sophisticated upgrade from the Mimosa. Slightly more alcoholic, the apricot brandy and orange bitters add a little extra complexity. The classy Valencia Cocktail No.2 makes an excellent addition to any cocktail party or elegant dinner.

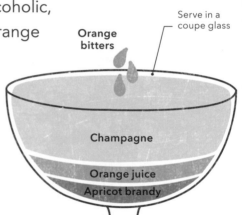

Orange bitters

Serve in a coupe glass

Champagne

Orange juice

Apricot brandy

## the CLASSIC RECIPE

This cocktail is a bubbly version of the Valencia Cocktail No.1.

1. Ensure all ingredients are chilled.
2. Pour 1 fl oz (30ml) apricot brandy into a glass.
3. Add ½ fl oz (15ml) orange juice and 3 drops of orange bitters.
4. Top with Champagne.

## EXTRAS

**Garnish:** Add an extra touch of elegance with a delicate orange twist.

# KIR ROYALE

Now considered a classic in its own right, the Kir Royale is a bubbly variation on a traditional French white wine cocktail, the Kir. Simple yet sophisticated, the Kir Royale consists of only two ingredients: crème de cassis and Champagne. Both recipes are named after Canon Felix Kir, a French priest who created the original Kir cocktail recipe. Elegant and easy to make, this cocktail makes the perfect dinner party aperitif.

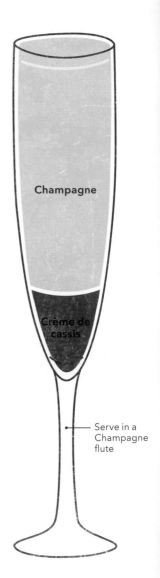

Champagne

Crème de cassis

Serve in a Champagne flute

## the CLASSIC RECIPE

The blackcurrant liqueur gives this cocktail a striking red color.

1. Pour ½ fl oz (15ml) crème de cassis into a Champagne flute.
2. Top with Champagne.

## EXTRAS

**Garnish:** Berries make an elegant garnish for this fruity drink.

TURN THE PAGE FOR REINVENTIONS ▶

LOSE the
BOOZE

**Swap the Champagne** for sparkling grape juice and replace the liqueur or brandy with fruit syrup.

# KIR ROYALE
## REINVENTED

### APRICOT ROYALE

A slightly sweeter, golden variation on the classic recipe.

1. Pour the apricot brandy into a Champagne flute.

2. Top with Champagne.

3. Garnish with a slice of fresh apricot.

Champagne

½ fl oz (15ml) apricot brandy

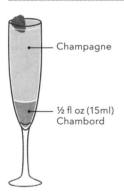

Champagne

½ fl oz (15ml) Chambord

### KIR IMPÉRIAL

A fun, pink twist with a subtly different flavor and slightly more booze.

1. Pour the Chambord into a Champagne flute.

2. Top with Champagne.

3. Garnish with a raspberry.

# OLD CUBAN

This modern classic, created in 2004 by Audrey Saunders, is essentially a minty daiquiri topped with fizz. If you're a fan of mojitos, this drink is a real game-changer. The name is a nod to the rum's Cuban heritage. For a lighter option, lose the rum and serve in a Champagne flute.

Serve in a coupe glass

Champagne
Simple syrup
Mint leaves
Lime juice
Golden rum

## the CLASSIC RECIPE

This cocktail brings out the best flavors of its simple ingredients.

1. Lightly muddle 6 mint leaves in a shaker.
2. Add 2 fl oz (60ml) golden rum, 1 fl oz (30ml) lime juice, and ½ fl oz (15ml) simple syrup.
3. Fill shaker with ice and shake for 15 seconds.
4. Double strain into a coupe glass.
5. Top with Champagne.

## EXTRAS

**Garnish:** Float a mint leaf in your drink for a delicate garnish.

TURN THE PAGE FOR REINVENTIONS ▶

# OLD CUBAN
## REINVENTED

### STRAWBERRY OLD CUBAN

A colorful twist, the pepper puts a kick behind the sweet strawberries.

1. Quarter the strawberries and muddle in a shaker.

2. Add the mint, rum, lime juice, and white pepper syrup.

3. Shake over ice for 15 seconds and double strain into a coupe glass.

4. Top with Champagne and garnish with a strawberry.

- 2 quartered strawberries
- Champagne
- 1/2 fl oz (15ml) white pepper syrup
- 1 fl oz (30ml) lime juice
- 2 fl oz (60ml) golden rum
- 6 mint leaves

- Champagne
- 1/2 fl oz (15ml) simple syrup
- 1 fl oz (30ml) lime juice
- 2 fl oz (60ml) golden rum
- 6 basil leaves

### BASIL OLD CUBAN

An equally delicious, slightly more savory alternative.

1. Combine the basil, rum, lime juice, and simple syrup in a shaker.

2. Fill shaker with ice and shake for 15 seconds.

3. Double strain into a coupe glass.

4. Top with Champagne and garnish with a basil leaf.

# AIRMAIL

First published in *Esquire Magazine*'s 1949 edition of "Handbook for Hosts," this delicious drink is named after the modern method of delivery by air—yet no one is quite sure where this association came from. A truly accessible cocktail, the rum and lime are softened by the citrusy orange and the sweetness of the honey.

## the CLASSIC RECIPE

Skip the rum for a delicious, low-alcohol alternative.

1. Add 1²/₃ fl oz (50ml) rum, ¹/₂ fl oz (15ml) lime juice, ¹/₂ fl oz (15ml) orange juice, and ¹/₃ fl oz (10ml) honey to a shaker.
2. Fill with ice and shake for 10 seconds.
3. Strain into a highball glass with ice.
4. Top with Champagne.

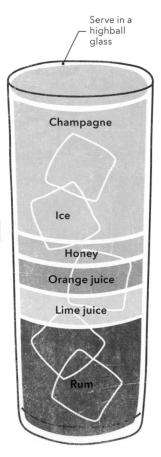

Serve in a highball glass

Champagne

Ice

Honey

Orange juice

Lime juice

Rum

## EXTRAS

**Garnish:**
Complete your
drink with a slice
of fresh orange
or lime.

TURN THE PAGE FOR REINVENTIONS ▶

# **AIRMAIL** REINVENTED

## **RUBY AIRMAIL**

This bold citrus and aromatic twist makes a great winter warmer.

1. Shake all ingredients except the Champagne over ice.

2. Strain into a highball glass with ice.

3. Top with Champagne and garnish with an orange twist.

3 drops cardamom bitters

Champagne

$^1/_3$ fl oz (10ml) pink grapefruit juice

$^1/_2$ fl oz (15ml) lime juice

$^2/_3$ fl oz (20ml) ruby port

$1^3/_5$ fl oz (50ml) rum

Champagne

$^1/_3$ fl oz (10ml) honey

$^1/_2$ fl oz (15ml) orange juice

$^1/_2$ fl oz (15ml) lime juice

$1^2/_3$ fl oz (50ml) tequila

## **TEQUILA AIRMAIL**

A simple spirit swap with zingy tequila instead of rum. This drink has a kick.

1. Shake all ingredients except the Champagne over ice.

2. Strain into a highball glass with ice.

3. Top with Champagne and garnish with a pink grapefruit twist.

# SGROPPINO

Light and enticingly easy to make, this classic Italian recipe is often served as a palate cleanser or even a replacement for dessert. The key ingredient is limoncello, a citrus liqueur made from lemons and largely produced in Sorrento, the Amalfi Coast, and Capri. With the tart citrus flavor, refreshing sorbet, and Mediterranean history, this cocktail is the perfect summer treat.

Prosecco

Lemon sorbet

Limoncello

Vodka

Serve in a coupe glass

## the CLASSIC RECIPE

The reaction between the sorbet and the fizz should make for a very bubbly drink.

1. Shake 1 fl oz (30ml) vodka and 1/3 fl oz (10ml) limoncello for 10 seconds over ice.

2. Add 1 scoop lemon sorbet to a coupe glass.

3. Strain liquid from the shaker over the sorbet.

4. Top with Prosecco.

## EXTRAS

**Garnish:** Give your drink an eye-catching pop of yellow with a sprinkling of lemon zest.

TURN THE PAGE FOR REINVENTIONS ▶

# SGROPPINO
## REINVENTED

### SAGE SGROPPINO

Both sorbets taste great with sage.

1. Shake the sherry and simple syrup over ice for 10 seconds.

2. Strain into a coupe glass with sorbet and top with Prosecco.

3. Garnish with a sage leaf.

Prosecco

1 scoop raspberry or pistachio sorbet

⅓ fl oz (10ml) simple syrup

1 fl oz (30ml) sherry infused with sage

Prosecco

1 scoop mango sorbet

⅓ fl oz (10ml) limoncello

1 fl oz (30ml) rum

### MANGO SGROPPINO

This one has summer written all over it.

1. Shake the rum and limoncello over ice for 10 seconds.

2. Strain into a coupe glass with sorbet and top with Prosecco.

3. Garnish with dried mango.

### RHUBARB SGROPPINO

A subtle, slightly sweeter twist.

1. Shake the vodka and rhubarb syrup over ice for 10 seconds.

2. Strain into a coupe glass with sorbet and top with Prosecco.

3. Garnish with lemon zest.

Prosecco

1 scoop lemon sorbet

⅓ fl oz (10ml) rhubarb syrup

1 fl oz (30ml) vodka

# ORGEAT FIZZ

Nutty and zesty, this low-alcohol cocktail is a great alternative to the boozy French 75. The main ingredient, orgeat, is a nonalcoholic syrup made from almonds and orange flower water. This refreshing drink first made an appearance in *The Savoy Cocktail Book* and is still adored by many bars. It makes a delicious, light tipple for scorching summer days.

## the CLASSIC RECIPE

Choose this drink if you're looking for less alcohol and more flavor.

1. Add ½ fl oz (15ml) orgeat and 1 fl oz (30ml) lemon juice to a shaker.
2. Fill with ice and shake for 15 seconds.
3. Strain into a highball glass filled with ice.
4. Top with Cava.

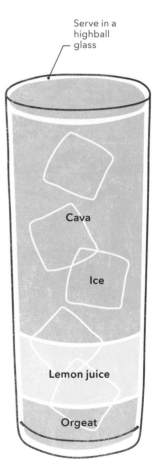

Serve in a highball glass

Cava

Ice

Lemon juice

Orgeat

## LOSE the
# BOOZE

**Substitute the Cava** for soda water to create a delicious nonalcoholic alternative to the classic recipe.

## EXTRAS

**Garnish:** Serve your drink to guests with an elegant lemon twist.

# SLOE GIN FIZZ

With gin's popularity on the rise, sloe gin is also enjoying its time in the spotlight. The deliciously fruity, tart liqueur is made by infusing sloe berries in gin and has been produced in the UK for hundreds of years. The most famous of its cocktails, the frothy Sloe Gin Fizz, was invented in the early 20th century. Berries, booze, and bubbles—what's not to like?

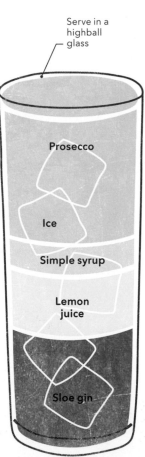

Serve in a highball glass

Prosecco

Ice

Simple syrup

Lemon juice

Sloe gin

## the CLASSIC RECIPE

The tart gin and lemon juice are balanced by sweet Prosecco and syrup.

1. Add 1²/₃ fl oz (50ml) sloe gin, 1 fl oz (30ml) lemon juice, and ¹/₂ fl oz (15ml) simple syrup to shaker.

2. Fill with ice and shake vigorously for 15 seconds.

3. Strain into highball glass filled with ice.

4. Top with Prosecco.

## EXTRAS

**Garnish:** Jazz up your drink with lemon zest or a lemon twist.

TURN THE PAGE FOR REINVENTIONS ▶

# SLOE GIN FIZZ
## REINVENTED

### CHARLIE CHAPLIN

This pre-Prohibition cocktail was invented at the Waldorf Astoria Hotel in 1920.

1. Add the sloe gin, lime juice, apricot brandy, and simple syrup to a shaker.

2. Fill with ice and shake for 10 seconds.

3. Strain into a highball glass filled with ice.

4. Top with Prosecco and garnish with a slice of fresh apricot.

Prosecco
½ fl oz (15ml) simple syrup
½ fl oz (15ml) apricot brandy
⁴/₅ fl oz (25ml) lime juice
1¹/₅ fl oz (35ml) sloe gin

Prosecco
¹/₃ fl oz (10ml) simple syrup
½ fl oz (15ml) ruby port
½ fl oz (15ml) applejack
1 fl oz (30ml) pink grapefruit juice
1 fl oz (30ml) sloe gin

### TAKE IT SLOE

Inspired by the Jack Rose cocktail, this ruby number has a real kick to it.

1. Add the sloe gin, grapefruit juice, applejack, ruby port, and simple syrup to a shaker.

2. Fill with ice and shake for 10 seconds.

3. Strain into a highball glass filled with ice.

4. Top with Prosecco and garnish with a wedge of fresh pink grapefruit.

# SPARKLING FRENCH MARTINI

All the flavors of the popular cocktail with an extra sparkle. The French Martini was invented in 1980s New York and gets its name from the iconic glass shape and French raspberry liqueur. It is now one of the most popular cocktails worldwide.

Prosecco

Pineapple juice

Chambord

Vodka

## the CLASSIC RECIPE

This fruity drink would also work well by replacing the Prosecco with Lambrusco.

1. Add 1 fl oz (30ml) vodka, 1 fl oz (30ml) Chambord, and $^2/_3$ fl oz (20ml) pineapple juice to a shaker.

2. Fill with ice and shake for 10 seconds.

3. Strain into a martini glass.

4. Top with Prosecco.

Serve in a martini glass

## LOSE the
# BOOZE

**Shake pineapple** juice and five fresh raspberries over ice. Double strain and top with ginger ale rather than Prosecco.

## EXTRAS

**Garnish:**
Decorate your drink with raspberries or fresh pineapple.

# DEATH IN THE AFTERNOON

A nod to the Ernest Hemingway book of the same name, this drink was created by the author himself while he was vacationing in the Florida Keys in the 1930s. The cocktail combines two of his great loves—absinthe and Champagne. Simple but powerful, there's a reason Hemingway named the drink after this particular book!

## the CLASSIC RECIPE

This is an intense aperitif for more adventurous drinkers.

1. Place a sugar cube at the bottom of a small Champagne flute.
2. Add ½ fl oz (15ml) absinthe.
3. Slowly top with Champagne.

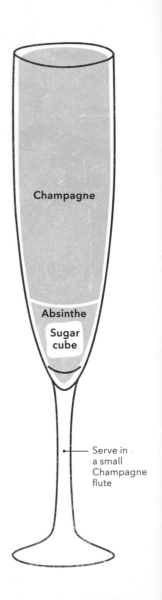

Champagne

Absinthe

Sugar cube

Serve in a small Champagne flute

## EXTRAS

**Garnish:** A twist of lemon gives some lift to this boozy aperitif.

TURN THE PAGE FOR REINVENTIONS ▶

LOSE the
BOOZE

**Replace the absinthe** with apple juice and top with soda water instead of Champagne.

# **DEATH** IN THE AFTERNOON
## REINVENTED

### **THE SUN ALSO RISES**

This effervescent, colorful showstopper is a fresh, floral twist on the original.

1. Place a sugar cube in the bottom of a small Champagne flute.

2. Add ½ fl oz (15ml) violet liqueur.

3. Slowly top with Champagne and garnish with edible flowers.

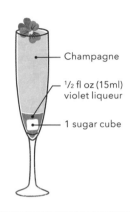

Champagne

½ fl oz (15ml) violet liqueur

1 sugar cube

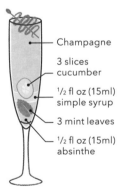

Champagne

3 slices cucumber

½ fl oz (15ml) simple syrup

3 mint leaves

½ fl oz (15ml) absinthe

### **THE DANGEROUS SUMMER**

A lighter drink for those who want to disguise the strong absinthe flavors.

1. Muddle cucumber in the bottom of a shaker. Add absinthe, simple syrup, and mint.

2. Fill shaker with ice and shake for 15 seconds.

3. Double strain into a small Champagne flute.

4. Top with Champagne and garnish with a cucumber swirl.

# SOUTHSIDE ROYALE

This is a bubbly variation on the Southside, a Prohibition-era drink with a mysterious history. Some say it originated in a New York speakeasy, The 21 Club. Others believe it emerged on the South Side of Chicago, where notorious gangs would compete with their North Side rivals selling cocktails made from illegal gin.

Champagne

Simple syrup

Mint leaves

Lemon juice

Gin

Serve in a coupe glass

## the CLASSIC RECIPE

This citrusy drink is traditionally served in a coupe glass.

1. Lightly muddle 6 mint leaves in a shaker.
2. Add 2 fl oz (60ml) gin, 1 fl oz (30ml) lemon juice, and ½ fl oz (15ml) simple syrup.
3. Fill shaker with ice and shake for 10 seconds.
4. Strain into a coupe glass.
5. Top with Champagne.

## LOSE the
# BOOZE
**This drink works** well replacing the gin with Seedlip and topping with ginger ale rather than Champagne.

## EXTRAS

**Garnish:**
Float a mint leaf in your cocktail for an elegant finish.

Exciting **cocktail creations** straight from the imagination of **Pippa Guy**, taking inspiration from cocktail-making **history** and experimentation with some of the most exciting **flavor combinations**. Try these if you want to serve something a little **different**—though you'd better start practicing, as they can be trickier to master!

# SOMETHING
# SPECIAL

# PINK TEQUILA FIZZ

If you're a fan of Margaritas and other tequila-based drinks, this one's for you. Taking inspiration from the Paloma, one of the most popular cocktails in Mexico, the Pink Tequila Fizz combines fresh pomegranate and hibiscus bitters to create a floral but zingy refresher.

## the AUTHOR'S RECIPE

The bright seeds add a burst of texture, color, and flavor.

1. Shake 1¹/₂ fl oz (45ml) tequila, ¹/₂ fl oz (15ml) pink grapefruit juice, ¹/₂ fl oz (15ml) lime juice, ¹/₂ fl oz (15ml) simple syrup, 3 drops hibiscus bitters, and the crushed seeds of ¹/₂ pomegranate over ice.

2. Strain the mixture into a highball glass filled with ice.

3. Top with rosé Champagne.

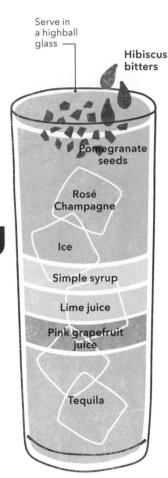

Serve in a highball glass

Hibiscus bitters

Pomegranate seeds

Rosé Champagne

Ice

Simple syrup

Lime juice

Pink grapefruit juice

Tequila

## EXTRAS

**Garnish:**
Rim the glass
with salt for
an extra kick.

SEE PP.48-49

# MIDSUMMER RUNNER

Created in celebration of summer, the sweet rhubarb and rose flavors lifted by the bubbles are such quintessential aromas of this season. With rum as the base spirit, the name is a nod to the mischievous rum runners of the 1920s.

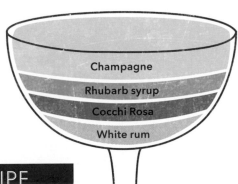

Champagne

Rhubarb syrup

Cocchi Rosa

White rum

Serve in a coupe glass

## the AUTHOR'S RECIPE

The flat coupe glass allows the aromas and beautiful pink hues to shine.

1. In a mixing glass with ice, combine 1 fl oz (30ml) white rum, 1 fl oz (30ml) Cocchi Rosa, and 1 fl oz (30ml) rhubarb syrup.

2. Stir for 20 seconds.

3. Strain into a coupe glass and top with Champagne.

# LEMONGRASS MULE

This sparkling nod to the Moscow Mule really brings the heat. Where the classic cocktail contains ginger beer, this fiery drink packs a punch with ginger syrup and lemongrass. Not for the faint-hearted! Like the Moscow Mule, this drink works well in a copper cup.

## the AUTHOR'S RECIPE

Add extra lemongrass purée to give your drink more of a kick.

1. Shake 1²/₃ fl oz (50ml) vodka, 1 fl oz (30ml) lime juice, ²/₃ fl oz (20ml) ginger syrup, and 1 tsp lemongrass paste over ice.
2. Strain into a highball glass or copper cup with ice.
3. Top with Champagne.

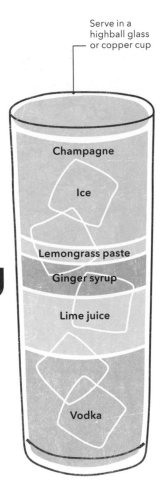

Serve in a highball glass or copper cup

Champagne

Ice

Lemongrass paste

Ginger syrup

Lime juice

Vodka

## LOSE the
# BOOZE

**Swap the vodka** for apple juice and replace the Champagne with soda water or sparkling grape juice.

## EXTRAS

**Garnish:** A fresh lemongrass stick makes a great garnish for this drink.

# ENGLISH SUMMER ROSE

This light, elegant, and floral drink goes down far too easily in the sun. The citrus and rose vodka infusion gives the flavor a real boost and complexity. The perfect crowd pleaser at a summer wedding or a picnic, why not try serving this to your guests in a punch bowl?

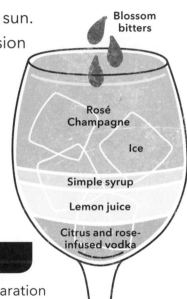

Blossom bitters

Rosé Champagne

Ice

Simple syrup

Lemon juice

Citrus and rose-infused vodka

Serve in a wine glass

## the AUTHOR'S RECIPE

This drink needs 2-3 hours of preparation to infuse the vodka (see pp.42-43).

1. Stir 1 fl oz (30ml) citrus and rose-infused vodka, 1 fl oz (30ml) lemon juice, ½ fl oz (15ml) simple syrup, and 3 drops blossom bitters in a mixing glass.

2. Strain into a wine glass filled with ice.

3. Top with rosé Champagne.

## EXTRAS

**Garnish:** Fresh or dried rose petals make a pretty and sophisticated decoration.

# ROYAL SILVER BULLET

This drink takes inspiration from the classic Silver Bullet cocktail, but the addition of Champagne adds a little extra fun. The slight sweetness of the Kummel comes forward, with the herbal caraway, cumin, and fennel lingering familiarly in the background.

Champagne

Lemon juice

Kummel

Gin

## the AUTHOR'S RECIPE

The elegance of this cocktail makes it a great choice for an evening drink.

1. Shake 1 fl oz (30ml) gin, ½ fl oz (15ml) Kummel, and ½ fl oz (15ml) lemon juice over ice.

2. Strain the mixture into a martini glass.

3. Top with Champagne.

Serve in a martini glass

## EXTRAS

**Garnish:** Silver leaf or edible silver glitter gives this drink an exciting, sparkly finish.

# CYNAR FIZZ

One for the more advanced cocktail maker and drinker. Made with the artichoke-based, herbal liqueur Cynar, this cocktail tests the palate with savory, nutty, and bitter tones. It has a heavier taste and texture than many fizz cocktails, so it is best served as an after-dinner digestif.

Serve in a small wine glass

Orgeat

Lemon juice

Cynar

Champagne

Egg white

## the AUTHOR'S RECIPE

Egg white binds the ingredients and leaves the drink with a creamy texture.

1. Shake 1 fl oz (30ml) Cynar, 1 fl oz (30ml) lemon juice, ½ fl oz (15ml) orgeat, and 1 egg white over ice.

2. Strain, then shake again without ice to get a good foam.

3. Pour a splash of Champagne into the bottom of the wine glass, then fill slowly with the cocktail.

## EXTRAS

**Garnish:** Crushed almonds add extra texture to this drink.

# INDEX